No Controversy

No Controversy

Celebrating the Life and Legacy
of SANDRA CLEMENTS

Dr. Kirby Clements Sr.

CLEMENTS
MINISTRIES

Decatur, GA

No Controversy: Celebrating the Life and Legacy of Sandra Clements

Address inquiries to the publisher:

Clements Family Ministries
2000 Cathedral Place
Decatur, Georgia 30034 USA

Learn more about the author and the ministry at www.clementsministries.org

ISBN: 978-0-9968702-3-8 (print)
ISBN: 978-0-9968702-4-5 (ebook)

Library of Congress Control Number: 2017963514

Edited and composed by Annette Johnson, Allwrite Communications Inc.
Cover by Q. J. Shepherd

Printed in the United States of America.

Table of Contents

Preface

My wife, Sandra, and I have always believed that Christianity is a supernatural faith. It is not rules, regulations and ordinances, but rather a living faith. God communicates with His people through His Word and Spirit. The gifts of the Holy Spirit are present and active today. Sandra and I received much ministry and life through the gifts of the Holy Spirit. We had a vision of a Bible encircled by light in 1976 while we were living in Duxbury, Massachusetts. We received two prophetic words in one day from different people while living in Maryland that addressed our future life and ministry. When we returned to Atlanta to begin our life and dentistry, we received numerous prophetic words from notable prophets about our call to the ministry. In fact, it was a prophetic word given to Sandra that promised her that the Lord would have the last word concerning her situation and medical challenges. And that prophetic word was the source of confidence for the Lord remembered the word upon which He caused us to hope. It has been this living and interactive faith that has sustained us.

This is a chronicle of the most significant events in our lives, effectively focusing on the last moments of Sandra's life and her legacy. It is a testimony to the grace and faithfulness of a covenant-keeping God. It is written after the life of my beloved Sandra. We were married for 50 years and she transitioned this life at the age of 71.

The title of book, *No Controversy*, was the phrase I used as I spoke over my beloved Sandra during her celebration service that Friday morning in June 2015. As I looked down upon the coffin that contained her beautiful body, so many thoughts filled my mind. I had never experienced this moment and the feelings of loss and separation were gradually becoming more apparent within me. I would never see my beloved Sandra or kiss her and tell her how much I loved her every day. We would not experience the fellowship of life together with all of its opportunities. We were together in every aspect of our existence including ministry and dentistry. Sandra was always there. She was a source of love, strength, encouragement, wisdom, and insight. She was spiritual, practical, and beautiful, and I loved her with all my heart. Relatives, friends and associates had gathered that morning. Our son, Kirby Jr., would eulogize his mother while our daughter, Gina, daughter-in-law, Suzette, and granddaughter, Gabrielle, would stir our hearts with their words. Bishop Bill Hamon, Dr. Carolyn Driver and Dr. Beverly Crawford would present their memories and perspectives of Sandra as well. Robert Childs Jr., Sandra's oldest brother, would express his love and appreciation for his sister.

As I pondered the last words that I would say over her that morning, I was overwhelmed with the thoughts of the faithfulness of the Lord in our lives. I took a moment and prayed in tongues. His grace was so evident during every phase of our lives and especially during all of the health challenges that Sandra experienced. We had been impressed for years that the Lord always has the last word in every situation. He contradicted the sentence of physicians, negated every negative prognosis, and prevented the side effects of numerous medications Sandra had taken for years. And during those last months of her life when the challenges became more and more evident, we were always impressed with the thought that His grace is sufficient.

The day before the final moment, Sandra and I were alone in the hospital room when she sat up and said, "The name, the name, the gate, the gate!"

We both were very much aware of the meaning of this experience. Even though I resisted the implications of that moment, I was powerless to change the time. And now, even though this moment was unwanted and unplanned, I can openly say that I had no controversy with the Lord. Thus, this brief chronicle will reveal the presence of His grace and mercy in the lives of Sandra and Kirby.

—Kirby Clements Sr.

CHAPTER 1

From the Beginning

We had known each other since Sandra was a senior in high school and I was a freshman in college. We had been married for over 50 years and are the parents of two wonderful children, Kirby Jr. and Gina, who, with their spouses, are the parents of Kirby III, Gabrielle, and Jeffrey Jr., respectively. Sandra and I had labored together in marriage, dentistry and in ministry. We had been inseparable in all things and been given the privilege to see parts of Africa, Asia, Australia, Europe, the Caribbean, the Netherlands, South America, and many parts of the United States during our ministry. Our commission was to be a husband-and-wife team because the *Spirit of the Lord was upon us and he had anointed us to preach the gospel to the poor, to set at liberty those who were bound, to heal the broken hearted and to declare the acceptable year of the Lord* (Luke 4:18). The Spirit had instructed us *to set in order the things that are wanting and ordain elders in every city* (Titus 1:5). The Spirit had encouraged us to *endure hardness as good soldier of Jesus Christ and not be entangled with affairs of this life so that we might please the one who enlisted us as soldiers* (2 Tim. 1:3-4). We received prophetic words concerning our life and ministry together. We were to co-labor, preach to the nations and write the things revealed to us about the Kingdom of God and the relationship between men and women in the home, church and marketplace.

Touch Not

Sandra had experienced numerous medical procedures and surgeries during our life together. In her book *Prevailing Spirit*, she recounted the many illnesses – some congenital – she suffered throughout her life, including asthma, myasthenia gravis, breast cancer, and thyroid disease. I was never absent from her side except during the surgeries. I slept in her hospital room in a chair next to her bed after every procedure she had ever experienced. I was vigilant in prayer and thanksgiving to the Lord, always asking if the physicians, technicians and nurses knew what to do and what not to do. The hand of the Lord had always been with us. In fact, one surgery was aborted supernaturally. Sandra had been prepared for open heart surgery when the surgeon felt strongly impressed to take another picture of her heart. To his surprise, he discovered a piece of plaque that would have been dislodged if he had done the surgery. He aborted the surgery before any incision was made. I remember when he came out to the waiting room where the children and I were waiting. The heart surgeon declared that we had just experienced a miracle. He described the entire event and how such surgeries can fail if plaque in a vessel is dislodged and it blocks a vessel.

Sandra was sent to recovery, and for the next six months, she was on medication. Then we discovered that the procedure needed for Sandra required a special skill. The Lord had stopped the hand of the surgeon because the surgeon He had assigned to the procedure was not yet in place. Even though the cardiologist who had attempted to operate was highly qualified, there was another surgeon who was not immediately available when Sandra needed her operation. When we met him shortly thereafter, he revealed to us that he had actually pioneered the specific surgical procedure that Sandra needed.

A similar incident had occurred years before when we left Atlanta, so I could attend dental school. Sandra had experienced chest pains for months without any proper diagnosis. Somehow, we were convinced that her medical treatment was not to occur in Atlanta, however. During my second year as a dental student and Sandra's position as a health care coordinator at very large hospital, President Nixon's personal surgeons freely provided her surgical care.

Sandra's graduation from Spelman College, holding Kirby Jr. alongside Kirby Sr.

CHAPTER 2

Prophetic Witnesses

Sandra and I believe that God is a communicator. He makes known His will for us individually and corporately through the Scriptures and the ministry of the Holy Spirit. Personal prophecy is a channel of Divine. It has been a tremendous source of edification, exhortation and comfort to us. When I finished my dental training in Washington, DC and we were preparing to move back to Atlanta, Sandra and I received prophetic words about ministry. We had desires in our hearts to serve the Lord and studied the Scriptures daily. There was neither a model for us to emulate nor was there anyone that we knew who could offer counsel regarding the merging of dentistry and ministry. But before we left Washington, two prophecies were given to us in the same day at different times. Both prophecies spoke of the desires that were in our hearts and that the Lord had set us in ministry.

Once we arrived in Atlanta, we joined a local church and started our dental practice. It was during the Word of Faith Movement and we attended a lot of the conferences that came to Atlanta. While attending several of the meetings, the speakers would publicly identify Sandra and I and say that we were called into the ministry. We already had desires in our hearts and had started a Bible study in our home. The prophecies gave meaning and stimulated faith in our hearts to launch out into the ministry.

We attempted to go to Bible college, but we were forbidden of the Lord. Still, we were students of the Scriptures, and we sat at the feet of some of the most notable teachers of that time. We grew in grace and in the knowledge of the Lord. Sandra and I were inseparable and always co-labored together. We held prayer meetings in our home, and we sponsored seminars. It was during those times that Sandra was impressed of the Lord with the issue of gender equality. We became a part of the pastoral staff of Chapel Hill Harvester Church, one of the first mega churches in America, and we labored in that ministry for 30 years while maintaining our dental practice, travelling and writing over 14 books. Throughout that time, Sandra and I experienced every challenge in life and ministry together.

International Ambassadors

As we travelled, we would often encounter prophets. We both served as members of the Board of Governors for Christian International with Bishop Bill Hamon, a notable prophetic voice in this country and the world. Prophetic words would often be given over us that stressed our unity and that God has made us "one flesh." During a retreat with the prophets, Sandra received a prophetic word that defined her as "God's ambassador for women" and that she would execute justice and bring hope to women and men in their effort to discover equality. One prophet spoke of the effectiveness of her life and ministry and how the Lord had fashioned us as a team. Sandra was indeed God's ambassador and her commitment to her studies was the catalyst for our many books written on creational order, including *And He Gave Them.*

We travelled to South Africa during the apartheid era and ministered throughout the country for a month. We spoke on the Kingdom of God and creational order. Sandra met with a large group of women of the Apostolic Faith Mission, and the experience was tremendous. She spoke on creational order and role of women in Scripture. The women wept uncontrollably as they listened to Sandra's teaching on co-laborship. The organization did not allow women to pastor and held firm to the male headship model. Thus, Sandra's message was revolutionary.

Sandra and I had traveled to Australia together. She had ministered on the Biblical rights of women and the senior minister of the church ordained three women after Sandra's teaching from the Scriptures. Her teachings were always Biblically based and practical. And because we co-labored together, the message of co-equality was stronger. Once during our teaching on creational order in England, the leadership of men requested that we not sell our new book at the time, *And He Gave Them,* and that we not speak any more on the topic.

Sandra's message on the equality, dignity, and role of women was so compelling and influential that the congregation was strongly affected. The wives of the elders were not allowed to teach or exercise any authority in the church. But when they heard and saw Sandra and I ministering together, there was a tremendous hunger in women for more of God. During one of the time of personal ministry in prayer for the congregation, the size of the crowd was too much for the elders, and Sandra and I requested the wives of the elders to assist us. The results were astonishing. Those women ministered with such authority and compassion, and many were healed of diseases, delivered from evil spirits and filled with the Holy Ghost.

Sandra was a diligent student of the Scriptures and read extensively. She kept her notes in a large leaf notebook. She was often invited to speak at conferences and churches on the topic of gender. Her knowledge of church history and the Scriptures always challenged and informed her audience. Sandra has a very extensive library of both historical and contemporary writings and books. It was her research and knowledge that served as the foundation for our first conference, which was called "The Gathering." We provided a most comprehensive collection of her writings and study notes. Each succeeding conference grew in content and attendance. In fact, we organized these seminars throughout the United States, South Africa, Europe, Asia, Caribbean, Curacao and Latin America. Our first published book entitled, *And He Gave Them*, is used as a text book in many churches and ministries.

As previously noted, T.L. and Daisy Osborn were world-renowned evangelists. They ministered in more nations and before the largest audiences of any known ministers. Daisy had a passion for the rights of women in the home, market place, and the church. She was strongly supported by her husband and her writings were a gift to Sandra. Their daughter, Bishop LaDonna Osborn, who followed in her parents' footsteps, said that the passion and call of the ministry of gender equality fell upon Sandra. She invited Sandra to be guest speaker with her on mission trips to Russia and Germany. I accompanied Sandra and witnessed the tremendous crowds of women and the effect of her ministry upon all that attended the conferences. Sandra's knowledge of the Scriptures and her teaching on history and the meaning of words such as head, helpmeet, authority, submission, silence, and covering thoroughly convinced the church.

Among the Prophets

It was during our time at Chapel Hill that Bishop Bill Hamon of the Christian International Ministry spoke prophetic words over us. One of the words spoken to Sandra served as a source of strength to us for over 35 years. Sandra was experiencing tremendous challenges in her body due to myasthenia gravis. The illness causes the muscles to weaken and caused Sandra to have difficulty in speaking, breathing, and walking at times. We had sought physicians, but the disease was deemed incurable. Sandra was taking large doses of steroids that caused her to gain weight. Bishop Hamon spoke to us on that one Tuesday evening in the company of the entire leadership and staff of Chapel Hill Harvester Church. He said that the last word had not been spoken concerning Sandra's condition and situation. God promised to do a miracle and it was coming forth. We rejoiced because Bishop Hamon had no knowledge of Sandra's condition. We recorded those prophetic words, and whenever Sandra was challenged by the illness, we remembered and rehearsed that word to ourselves. Paul reminded Timothy "to fight a good fight according to the prophecies that had been given to him" (1 Tim. 1:18). We were so grateful that the Lord remembered the word upon which He caused us to hope (Psalm 119:49-50). And that word served as the catalyst for hope for over 35 years.

Bishop Bill Hamon invited Sandra and I to serve on the Board of Governors of the Christian International Ministries. It still is a global organization used to promote the ministry of the saints and development of the prophetic. Sandra was a keen prophet and possessed tremendous discernment and insight. During the annual conferences of the organization, we would attend various group meetings where the gender issue would be discussed. Sandra's insight and knowledge of the Scripture was a tremendous resource. She openly presented the reasons for the misconception of female submission and male domination. Sandra's prophetic words were so precise and timely that even those who resisted her teaching would reconsider their positions.

Even now, my momentum continues and is sustained by prophetic words that we received over the years. We traveled to many nations, but the prophecies never said that I would go alone. Every prophecy given to us, I always applied it to the both of us. We were a team. Yet, I am now alone. The sadness, loneliness, and confusion sweeps over me like waves at times. Sandra is no longer boarding the plane and sitting next to me for those long trips. We do not physically stand before the people in different nations and teach on the Kingdom of God and creation order. I now go alone. However, Sandra remains with me in my heart and in my mind. Whenever and wherever I minister, I will minister some for Sandra. I will stay true to our Divine agenda to set in order the things that are lacking and ordain elders in every city (Titus 1:5). I will remember that the Spirit of the Lord is upon me and He has anointed me to preach the gospel to the poor; to open the prison doors created by culture; to heal those bruised by discrimination and oppression; and to declare that this is the day of their deliverance (Luke 4:18). I will still proclaim and demonstrate His word and power. Our children are called of God because our ministry is a family ministry. That has not changed. Sandra is present mentally even though she is absent physically. And we thank the Lord that He remembers the prophetic words to us that continue to stimulate hope in our hearts.

Ministry trip to South Africa, 1987

Visiting the Dutch Reformed Church in South Africa

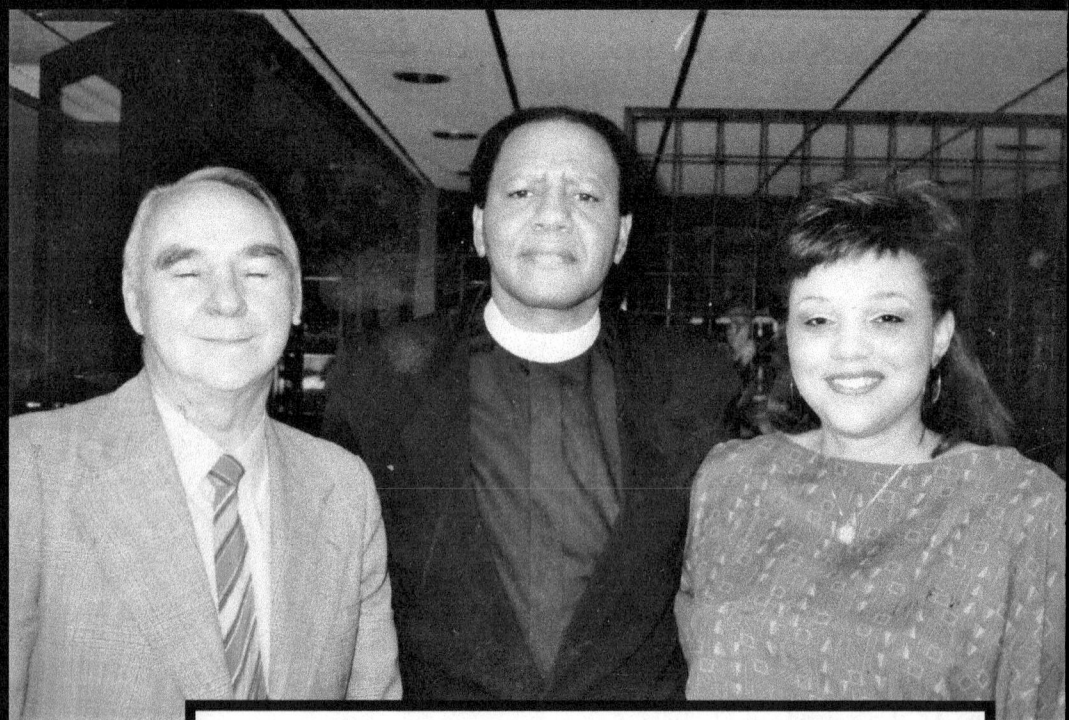

Day 2 at the Dutch Reformed Church

Sandra and Kirby Sr. at a conference in South Africa, 1988

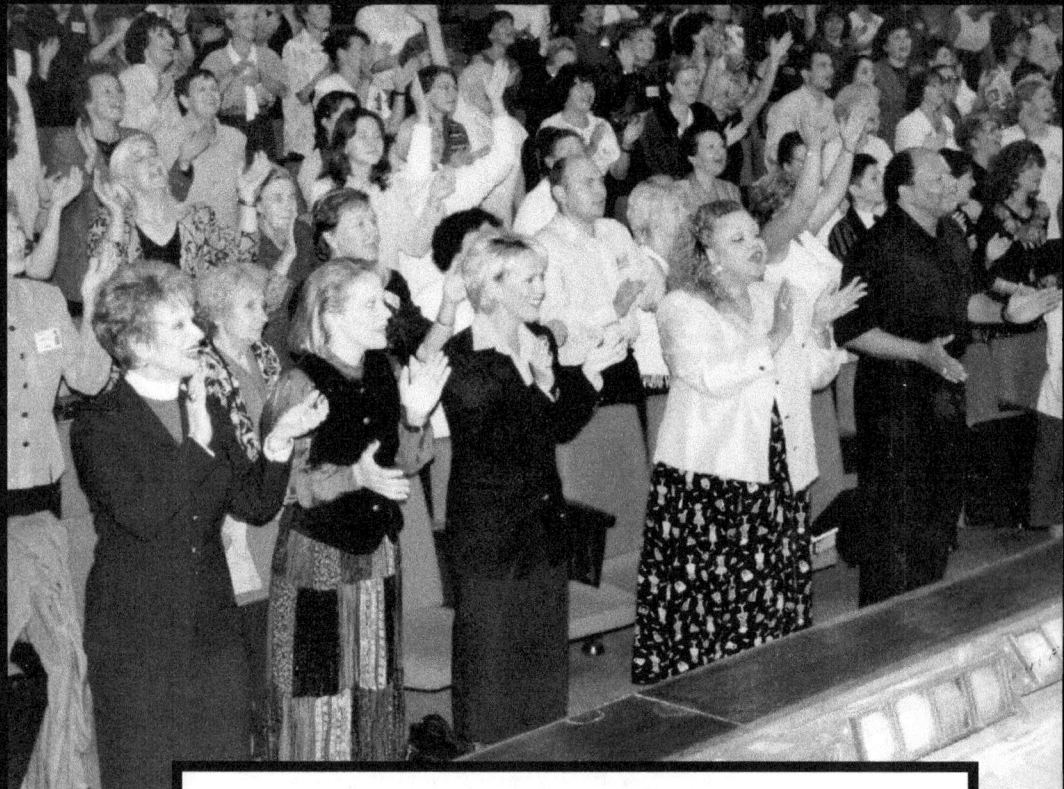

Women's conference in Moscow, Sept. 2000

Ministry team in Curacao, December 2004

Ministry team in Estonia, 2012

CHAPTER 3

And Now

As I sat vigilant beside Sandra's bedside each night, she would occasionally say things that she had never mentioned. One night as we sat in silence, she proclaimed, "The name, the name, the gate, the gate." I was startled, but I knew she was experiencing another realm. In fact, while the children were present, she mentioned the name of her departed sister and said for her to open the door. I knew that when the time of departure from this life was near, such experiences would occur. I had witnessed the same experience with my mother before she passed. There was no distress in Sandra's announcement, but there was a strong sense of reality. Sandra was being permitted to pierce the thin veil that separates this seen and physical world from the world that is unseen and spiritual. When she mentioned the gate, I was angry at the announcement and openly declared that we were not coming. Still, I knew that I was powerless to resist the will of the Lord. His will is always done.

And now, after over 50 years of co-laboring together, my Sandra was no longer in this world. The children, grandchildren and I surrounded her that June 13, 2015. Each one of us prayed and gave thanks to the Lord for her life. Each of us spoke to her with wonderful words of thanksgiving and praise for her influence and meaning in our lives. We prayed and spoke to her of our love. We looked upon her beautiful clay form, but she was not there. She had slipped away quietly without distress. When we left her beautiful form there in that hospital bed, it was the most difficult thing that I have ever done in my life. We were all in a daze as we gathered our belongings and began to walk out of the room. We glanced back to look upon her once again before finally leaving. We all drove home in separate cars while our daughter, Gina, and her son, Jeffrey Jr., rode with me.

There had been no pain or desperation during this experience. I had been by her bedside since we entered Emory University Hospital on Friday, June 6, along with Kirby Jr., Suzette, Gina, Kirby III, Gabrielle, Jeffrey Jr., and Kala. We talked with her, held and kissed her, and cared for her that entire week. Each of us expressed our love and spoke to her about her meaning in our lives. During the week, all of our extended family and close friends came to visit. Occasionally, she would sit up and speak to us. Once, she spoke out loudly to the children to fight. This was a true mother of faith challenging her children to live in a world that she would no longer inhabit. Now she is in the presence of the Lord.

There had been no pain or desperation during this experience. I had been with her during every medical appointment and treatment she experienced over 50 years. I slept by her bedside in the hospitals every night that she was there. But this privilege would not be given to me anymore. There would be no more medical appointments and no more hospital visits. She would no longer have to count out thirty-seven pills and supplements every day. All the medical support and medication that had helped for so many years was no longer necessary. She was so peaceful and so beautiful and we looked upon her and we cried. We had never experienced this before and we had no idea of the dimensions of this moment upon our lives.

I remember the fear, dread, grief, and the regret that gripped my heart the morning the children and I came home after leaving her body at the hospital. And as I entered our bedroom that morning, anxiety and desperation seemed to overwhelm me like floods of unexpected water. She was not there, and she would not be close to me as she had been for those 50 years. I would no longer be able to kiss her and talk about all the issues of life. We would no longer plan ministry trips or conferences again. I could smell her fragrance as I walked into our closet and saw her beautiful clothes. As I looked around our bedroom, my mind was attempting to comprehend life without her. It was still too early to comprehend all my thoughts and emotions. Loneliness and grief were and still are new to me.

Our pattern for years was for me to go and open the office early on Saturday, and my sister, Melody, our hygienist, would pick up Sandra and drive to the office before 8 a.m. We would never experience our routine again. I would not hear her joyful voice as she entered the office. We would not work as a team and she would no longer manage all the affairs of the office. We had co-authored over 14 books, but her passion was revealed in two: *And He Gave Them,* a book that presents a Biblical foundation for the co-equality, co-essentiality and co-substantiality of women, and *Her Name is Mother,* a book that chronicles her concepts of parenting. She had written a final book titled *Prevailing Spirit,* which records her struggles and triumphs over the many health challenges, but she would not be present to see it released in August 2016.

During this first week after her transition, I was alone with my thoughts and memories. However, I choose not to cancel any appointments for ministry or dentistry. In fact, the same morning after her transition, I treated patients at our dental practice that morning and ministered in our local church that evening. I committed myself to some degree of continuity knowing that to discontinue my patterns would have grave consequences. I knew grief and anxiety would pour over my soul like waves and engulf me without warning.

The Void

Still, there is a void in our family's lives that is foreign to us. The dimension of our world has been radically diminished. The grief, sense of loss, and even panic seem to consume us at times. It comes upon us unannounced while we are simply speaking or walking about. The landscape of our lives has changed. And now I cannot call Sandra many times during the day just to hear her voice and see how she is doing. I can no longer kiss her three times when I leave for a trip, the office or simply to run an errand. I can no longer hold her hand or open the door of the car for her. As I walk through our house, I see her signature on all the pictures and furniture. When I enter my dental office, I go alone because she is no longer here to walk in and administrate the practice as she has done for over 35 years. Melody would always bring her to the office on Saturday since I would leave early to set up. When Sandra would enter the office, she would always greet us in Spanish, saying, "Cómo estás? (How are you doing?)"

Panic grips my mind when I think of life without my Sandra. Pain and grief engulfs my soul when I think of traveling to places we visited together. I often ask myself, *What will I do without her? How can I manage our life at home, office, and church?*

Indeed, I generated the income while Sandra managed all of the affairs, and she did it wonderfully. She had been my confidant, companion, and my resource in life. We travelled to Asia, Africa, Australia, Europe, South and North America together. We ministered as a team. We had shared everything together, but now she is gone. We will no longer ride in the car to doctors' appointments or take trips to the mall or restaurant. I no longer sit and sleep on the unfolding chair in the hospital room all night and everyday as I had when she was a patient. I can no longer experience the joy and happiness when she would be released from the hospital.

Without her, there is no "we." We can no longer sit on the front porch or in the cathedral room or in the Florida room of our home and talk about the ministry or life issues. We can no longer have family dinners with Kirby Jr., Suzette, Gina and their children at our home as we've done for many years. We can no longer pray together on every Friday morning during the time we had established for the church. We can no longer wake early in the morning and talk for hours about everything while sitting in bed. We can no longer ask one another questions about the Scriptures. I can no longer be given the privilege to encourage her and communicate impressions I received of the Lord when I come up from downstairs after a time of study, writing, and prayer early in the morning. She is no longer here to ask me, "What did the Lord say today?"

Oh, how I miss her innocence and trust in the words and impressions of the Lord, for they would often be the answers to her concerns and questions. I can no longer have the opportunity to encourage us both with biblical proclamations, decrees, and words of wisdom, including "The Lord has the last word" or "What He has said, He has said, and what He has done, He has done." I can no longer have the opportunity to recite how the Lord stopped the hand of a surgeon who had prepped Sandra for open heart surgery. No longer can I say how the Lord has contradicted every negative prognosis and negated the negative side effects of medication.

The Children

Our children, Kirby Jr. and Gina, have been trying to manage the loss of their mother. Each of them had a special bond with her. They have so many memories of their times with their mother. After all, Sandra and I had personally been there during every phase of their social, spiritual, and educational journey until they graduated from law school. Sandra and Gina had searched for a beautiful gown in preparation for Gina's wedding. In fact, Gina chose the same dress her mother wore for her wedding as the dress for Sandra's final celebration. How often the children had come into our bedroom and sprawled across the bed and talked endlessly with their mother about all their life issues. And now, Sandra was no longer here to answer their phone calls or even to call them. She would no longer call or text each of them just to see how they are doing or to make a request.

Sandra and I had been doting grandparents and very involved in the lives of our grandchildren Kirby III, Gabrielle and Jeffrey Jr. Kirby III lived with us for almost a year when he was 2 years old while his mother, Dr. Suzette Clements, went to New York to begin her medical training. Now the children and grandchildren are navigating life without mother and grandmother. Gina's husband, Jeffrey Sr., cried during the celebration and openly expressed to Gina his feelings of loss and sorrow over Sandra's transition. All of us were wrestling with our thoughts, grief, and our fears.

None of us is angry, though. We had not anticipated this end of life and such a radical change in our world. The landscape of our lives changed, and we did not see it coming. I personally felt that there were years ahead of us and that there were nations that we were to visit for ministry. And now, I pour through all the pictures, recordings and videos just to get a glimpse of my Sandra and to hear her voice.

We are comforted by the fact that Sandra did not suffer or experience pain during her last days on this earth. She was filled with hope and confidence that she would recover from this challenge. She and I discussed these thoughts endlessly as I sat vigilant by her bedside the entire time of her hospitalization. There were never any moments of hopelessness, fear or anxiety. We felt that life and ministry were continuing ahead of us. After all, we had only known life for 54 years together. Perhaps our experiences can be a source of encouragement, strength and hope to others. We have no controversy with the Lord and we never once asked, "Why?"

...rby Sr. and Sandra with Kirby Jr. graduating from Emory Law School, May 1990

...andra with granddaughter Gabrielle, May 2012

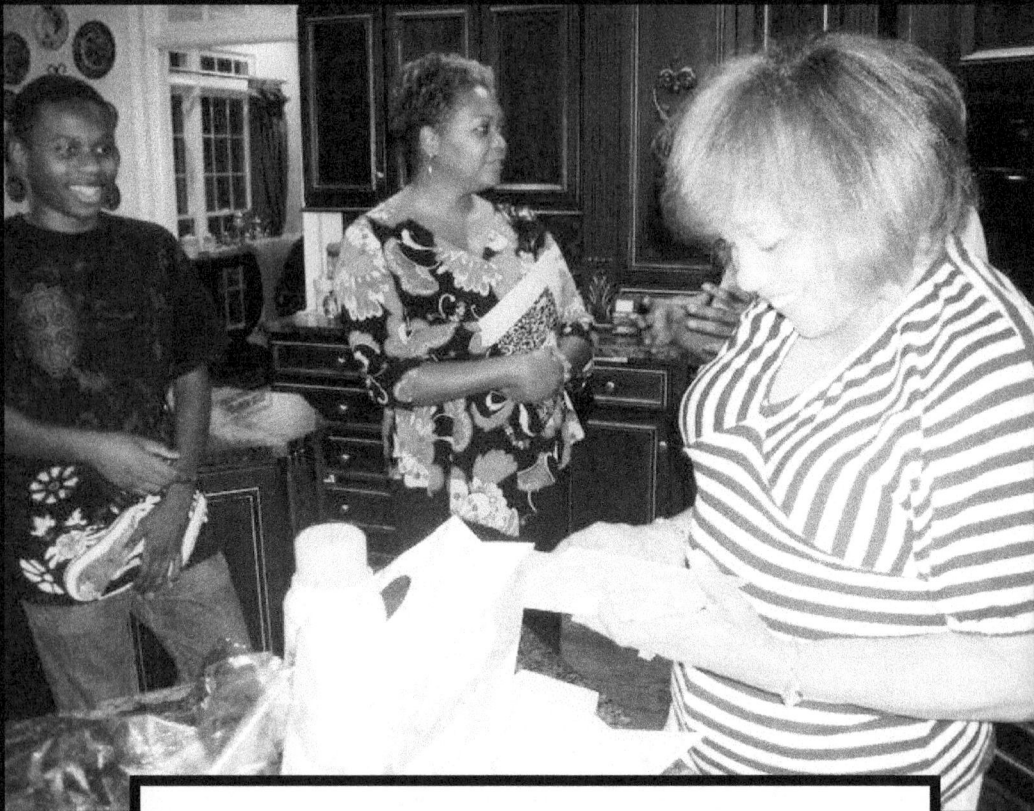

Celebrating Sandra's 70th birthday, July 4, 2014

andra with Gina and her husband, Jeffrey Sr., nd Jeffrey Jr.

Sandra with Jeffrey Jr. at the strawberry patch, May 2014

CHAPTER 4

His Grace is Sufficient

Sandra had expressed her desire to us that if any life threatening event occurred that she did not desire any emergency procedures to resuscitate her. She was spared of any radiation or chemo-treatment. The medical team at the hospital provided exceptional and tender care during her time there. We, as a family, are impressed with the thought that the grace of the Lord was sufficient for Sandra. His grace was so amazing, as it was expressed in Divine favor, strength, courage, and confidence.

During the days after Sandra's transition, I would often say that we have no controversy with the Lord. How could we blame God for such mercy and grace? As my mind searched the unlimited memories of Divine intervention in our lives and the numerous times His healing love had rescued us, how could I blame God? No, the Lord received Sandra because in His sovereignty, this was her time. It was not one second, minute, hour, day, week, month or year before the time.

How often during such times has the Lord been blamed for prematurely taking a life to heaven? I had personally witnessed funeral services where the ministers would claim that the Lord took the life of the person being eulogized because there was a need in heaven. No, the Lord does not take anyone but, rather the Lord receives them. Many times during the public services for Sandra, I would declare that we had "no controversy." This statement was a tremendous source of healing for many people who had lost loved ones. A mother had recently lost her son and was in great pain and despair. She was angry with the Lord because she had been told by her minister that the Lord took her son. She came to me and proclaimed her own healing when she heard me say, "We have no controversy with the Lord."

He Hid This from Us

After Sandra's transition, her physicians began to call. Their final reports were simply the problem had not been detected despite all of the modern technology and medical expertise. It seemed as if this issue had been hidden from them. In fact, the oncologist called and confided that none of the comprehensive test revealed this. Furthermore, if they had detected this, the treatment would have been too challenging for Sandra. The Lord spared Sandra the trauma, and His grace is sufficient.

The prophet declared that the death of the son of the Shulamite woman had been hidden from him. This experience of the prophet had great meaning to me and the children. Not once was our faith and hope of the recovery of Sandra dampened. We embraced the thought of her coming home in strength and health. In fact, the conclusive diagnosis was not discovered and made known until 24 hours before Sandra transitioned. But it became painfully clear that this experience had been hidden from us. In retrospect, there had been impression in my mind of being alone without Sandra. Often when I was driving the car or sitting at my desk in my office, I would have a glimpse of life without Sandra. I would resist the thought and substitute it with other memories of us together. For two years ago, I felt strongly encouraged to record and learn the things that Sandra did to keep the home, office, and the church going. She was a tremendously gifted person with administrative skills. Sandra was very discerning of people, times and seasons and she knew what needed to be done. She was a problem solver and could very quickly resolve some of the most challenging issues. Sandra and I recognized our individual gifts, and we functioned in them. Because of this, she managed the financial affairs for the home, dental practice, and the ministry. Two years ago, she and I had sat down and discussed all of these matters. I was reluctant to have such a discussion since it remind-ed me of taking the last will and testament of an individual before their demise. I was not happy to ask about insurance policies and where certain documents were recorded and stored. However, I obeyed the admonition, and we created an administrative workbook for the home, office, and ministry. I am glad that we did.

This Is the Day the Lord Has Made

The Lord had allowed me and our children to be there during the moment when Sandra transitioned. Her passing was no accident, and there was no negligence or mistake in medical treatment. Sandra and I have always been very attentive to our health. We had always been diligent to care for our bodies and get regular medical care. There was rarely a week over the last 30 years that we did not have at least one or two medical appointments. In fact, in the last two months of her life, I had admitted her three times to the emergency room for treatment. Each time, a battery of tests, x-rays, scans and blood work was done. None of the tests revealed anything definitive, however. The physicians were indecisive as to her diagnosis. They mentioned congestive heart failure, myasthenia gravis or asthma. I firmly believe that the Lord hid her condition from them. If they had initiated some treatment, then the diagnosis would have been confirmed. We would have been faced with a terrible diagnosis for the last weeks of her life. Again, the grace of the Lord hid this from our eyes. I firmly believe that to live with hope is more joyful than to live with hopelessness. The Lord gave Sandra and us all grace of hope, for the final diagnosis did not come until a few hours before she departed. The Lord had designed the time and the circumstances of Sandra departure. Again, we have no controversy with the Lord.

Taking a walk at home and admiring some of Sandra's favorite things, the flowers

At home on July 4, 2010

Enjoying Sandra's 70th birthday lunch

Enjoying time together at home

Christmas 2012

Christmas 2014

Ordaining new leaders with longtime ministry partn[...]
Pastor Dan Rhodes and his wife

CHAPTER 5

Final Words

For Sandra's funeral, which we deemed as "a celebration" of her life, I asked Kirby Jr., Gina, and Suzette to express their sincere feelings and impressions. Each of them spoke from the heart, even though the pain of loss would engulf them at times. This moment affected my daughter-in-law, Suzette, in a profoundly personal way. She had not brought closure to the death of both her parents, for she was not with them when they transitioned. The experience of all of us surrounding Sandra and worshipping the Lord in prayers and thanksgiving allowed her to bring closure to a chapter of her life that had been incomplete for many years. God was so good to us that day.

A few days before celebrating her legacy, our daughter Gina prepared her mother's hair and applied her makeup, as she had done so many times before. Our Sandra looked so radiant as Gina,

Kirby Jr., Suzette, and I looked upon her beautiful body lying so calm. She was beautiful and radiant in this state as she had always been. Our son, Kirby Jr., eulogized his mother like no one else could. Bishop Dale Bronner of Word of Faith Church presided wonderfully. Dr. Beverly Crawford spoke on the dignity of womanhood, Bishop Hamon spoke on the power of the Spirit, Dr. Carolyn Driver spoke on the significance of friendship, Gina and Sue spoke on the relationship of mother and daughter, Gabrielle spoke on grandmother and grandchildren, and I spoke on the power of covenant. Many people from near and far came to worship the Lord with us and to speak of the influence of my Sandra upon their lives and the world.

These are the precious words spoken during Sandra's homegoing service:

Our Son Eulogizes His Mother

First, I used to feel my mother. It conflicts with my natural logical mind, but I have come to accept that I could feel her. Oddly, I felt the negatives. I felt her pain, sadness, sometimes anger. I used to wonder why my shoulder or hip or other body part would hurt and then I would call her and in conversation I'd learn that she was having that same pain in the same place. Sometimes I would feel sadness or depression and when I would talk with her, she'd tell me that she had been feeling that way. I used to resist believing that I could feel her, but time after time, I did. In addition, I felt the connection. If I could put it in words that you could understand I would say it this way, imagine having your eyes closed and yet being able to sense when someone stood beside you. Now make that feeling more faint, but still clear. That's how I felt. I remember in the last days, before we knew it was the last days, we were discussing her breathing difficulty issues. We were all telling her things to help her and I told her how she should think. I told her to take each moment as it came and not to look at each new difficulty as a continuation of the old one and instead to focus only on the issue as it arose, this way her anxiety would not increase. She told me that my words spoke exactly how she felt and helped her to deal with the challenges. I have never had breathing problems, so how did I know exactly how she was feeling? It was our connection.

I was also painfully aware that I was also not able to feel my mom towards the end of her life. I did not feel breathing issues, with the exception of once where I felt like I was not getting enough air, but that was so brief as not to even count. I did not feel her difficulty like I felt the others. I used to have chest pain when she had it, in the same place and could describe it the same way. I never had heart problems. I used to have random aches when she had them, where she had them, and in the same manner, but now, I could not feel my mom. When she entered the hospital for the final time, I had knowledge of things that she was feeling and she articulated those things, but I did not feel them. I felt the loss of her while she was still here. It was scary, it was saddening, but it was clear. I knew that things were different. I even remarked to my son before she went into the hospital what my feelings were about her life expectancy. It was based entirely upon what I could feel, could see, and could not feel. I do feel differently now. I don't feel her anymore. I am very aware of it. If I were to describe it to you, I'd say, imagine laying in your bed and feeling the bed, now when you get up, you no longer feel the bed. Normally, you don't think about it, but imagine if you were ordinarily aware of the feeling of the bed and now you are aware of its absence. Put another way, I can feel that I can't feel her. But that is not because she no longer exists.

During her eulogy, I told everyone two things that came to me as I had prepared to eulogize my mom. First, in the span of our human existence, we have never understood the next level of our existence. The sperm and egg did not contemplate what it meant to be a fetus. They just fulfilled their purpose and then a new form of existence started. The fetus did not contemplate what it meant to be a fully autonomous being, getting an education, a family, a job, or anything. It only knew what its existence was. Once born, we matured and we understood all the past parts of our existence, but in the end, we could only fulfill our purpose on earth but could not fully comprehend our next level of existence. People often say that our loved ones are doing in heaven the same thing they did here on earth. That is because we can only comprehend life as we know it. Jesus said that no one is married or given in marriage in heaven, so clearly the concept of being reunited with a loved one in the same manner would seem out of the question. Still, there is a next dimension to our existence.

I say that there is a next dimension because life is a gift from God. In Genesis, it says that he breathed life into his creation. His essence came into us who were made in His likeness. His gifts are without repentance. He sent his son to redeem us. Clearly, that was for more than the short duration of our life here in this dimension. In short, my mom experienced life before me that made her into the woman that I knew. She experienced life with me and I enjoyed every minute of it, and she continues.

Graceful Words of Our Daughter

My mother was not only my mother, but my best friend. She was my confidant, my ride-or-die mom, my biggest cheerleader, and encourager. She instilled in us to serve the Lord, that he was our foundation, and our supplier. She told us that she would pray that the Lord kill us if we did not serve him. I use to say "death", why death, and she would say "If you don't serve him, you're already dead." She taught me to pray. She taught me how you give thanks to the Lord, and that you just do not pray to get, but you pray to give thanks and praise. I remember receiving the Baptism of the Holy Spirit when I was 8 years old sitting on the floor of our dining room in our house in Southwest Atlanta. Mom led me. She taught us about the Bible, and made sure it was in our hearts. She used to make Kirby and I read the Bible to her religiously before we could play. Because of that we knew the Word, because it was in us, in addition, I learned to read out loud very well.

She was a strong proponent of education. She told Kirby and I from an early age that we would go to college, and graduate in 4 years, not 5. And if we graduated in 5 years, we would have to pay for the 5th year. Needless to say I graduated in 4 years. In addition, she told us that that we would obtain a graduate degree. She did not care what it was in, but she said that we had to obtain one. I was an overachiever, and obtained two, a Master's degree, and a Juris Doctorate. She believed in me and knew that I would exceed, and with that I have.

Family was very important to her, and she instilled the same in us. It was always the 4 of us before Kirby and I got married to our spouses. We did everything together, and when Kirby got married it was the three of us. I traveled with them national and internationally when I would be home from school, and during the years in between me obtaining my degrees. Those are memorable and precious times that I will forever cherish. I lived with them well into my 30's, not because I wanted too, but because my Dad proclaimed that I came in with a certificate, a birth certificate, and I would leave with a certificate, a marriage license. I would tell Mom how much I wanted my own home, and she went house hunting with me on many occasions, just because I asked. I did get my wish, when Mom and Dad moved out of the house into their new home. Mom was happy for me. Looking back, those were wonderful times, having her just down the hall. I would not have changed it for the world. During those times, she made birthdays, holidays, graduations, and births memorable. She would bring all of us together. That meant extended family, and friends too. Christmas was always wonder-

ful. Family, food, a huge Christmas tree, decorated Mom-style with lights in the windows, poinsettia's everywhere, and gifts wrapped to match the color of the Christmas tree. No Christmas décor was ever the same. Everyone would bring their gifts to later be announced by my Dad, or Kirby, but only after we expressed our gratitude to the Lord for what He'd done for us, singing Christmas carols and getting lost in the "12 Days of Christmas". Ultimately, ending the evening with just the Clements' and the Boyd's. Easter was the same, Easter egg hunts for the kids, with decorations to match, and games for the children. It was always a joyous time, with family and friends.

She put family first in all she did. She loved us unconditionally, and would do anything she could for us, no matter what. She was truthful with us, she never lied to us, she was open, kind and loving. She listened, amidst her health challenges she pushed herself for us. I remember she shopping with me for vases for my wedding center-pieces. Week after week she would go with me, and helped me plan the wedding of my dreams. She believed us, she trusted us, and she instilled character, integrity, and fortitude in us. She is the reason I am the person I am today: the daughter, sister, wife, mother and friend.

I miss her more than words can say. I told her once that I did not know how I could make it if she ever died. She said to me, "You'll make it." She knew that because of what she instilled in me. She did not say to me how hard it would be experiencing the loss of her, but she said that I would make it. Her absence is so great in my life that it takes my breath away when I think that she is gone. I cannot fully conceptualize her death because if I do, it will be more than I can handle, but what I do is I remember all the wonderful memories that I have, I look at her pictures, I talk about her, and think of the funny things she would say and do. I laugh, I cry, my heart aches, but as my Dad has said "His grace is sufficient for us." I will say that I have no regrets, because during my lifetime, I said everything I had to and needed to say to my Mother, that was the nature of our relationship.

Thank you, Sandra Childs Clements, for your uncondi-tional love, for the example you exemplified as a great Wom-an of God, wife, sister, aunt, grandmother, friend, and mother. I love you Mother, your most gracious daughter, G.

Wonderful Words of a Daughter

Next, Suzette spoke of Sandra during the celebration. Her words echoed such great love, honor and respect. This what Su-zette said regarding Sandra:

The days of your life were threescore years and 10. Well done, thou, good and faithful servant. Well done! You lived with your heart wide open and taught us to be people of integrity, faith and family. You embodied Christ and allowed the Holy Spirit to shine in and through you as a vessel of wisdom, stability and a woman of authority. You trusted in the Lord and leaned not to your own understanding. In all your ways you acknowledged him and he di-rected your path. You rose again and again despite your many chal-lenging physical illnesses and prove God to be your Jehovah Rapha, the healer. You planted the seeds of greatness in us while you stood as the mighty Oak. You did everything on a grand scale, and you mothered us all the same, making you truly a "Grand Mother." You, like the Paraclete, was one sent alongside to help, and you did so with conviction, compassion and joy.

We shared so much in common:

1) *Our initials are SC*

2) *Our children's initials are KC and GC*

3) *We are both married to Kirby Clements*

4) *We both have sons named Kirby Clements*

5) *We loved to garden and motivate our husbands to choose healthy habits, i.e. limiting The Varsity and getting their minds right.*

6) *Our husbands are our best friends.*

You knew what you wanted out of life, and you lived life to the fullest. You are truly a Grand Mother. Your words carried much weight and useful life into the masses. When we first met, he told me you wanted your grandchildren to call you grandmother. Only one problem, you didn't tell me what you wanted me to call you. So I call you: faithful, loving, committed, discerning, compassionate, caring, dedicated, wise, enlightened, trailblazer and a divine spiritual being that did everything on a "Grand Scale", making you a true "Grand Mother".

As your earthly life drew nigh, you tried to tell us but we didn't want to believe. Thank you for speaking what you wanted and didn't want at the hospital. You instructed us not to put you on a ventilator it needed and we listened. You instructed us not to resuscitate you if your heart stopped and we listened. Once again, just as you live knowing what you wanted, you died knowing what you wanted. Your courage to face death straight on made your transition somewhat easy to accept. Thank you for your awesome bravery.

I am honored to have known your beautiful spirit that influenced us all so mightily because you knew what you wanted out of life and death. Christmas and Easter will always be synonymous with you Sandra Clements. I do not say goodbye for I know to be absent from the body is to be present with Christ.

I ask that if you continue wearing those high heels in heaven, please let God know that as your podiatrists, I do not consent on earth or even in heaven. I love you deeply and will always see your beautiful smile in the eyes of a child, your strength in the tall oak tree, smell your fragrance in the blooming flowers and your innocence in the morning dew.

*May your book, Her Name is Mother, become a New York Times bestseller and exponentially spread your Christ-like wisdom on motherhood. By the way, your book's title should really have been her name is **Grand** Mother with grand in bold.*

Thanks for being an amazing part of my journey. May the road rise up to meet you. May the wind be always at your back. May the sun shine warm upon your face; the rains fall soft upon your fields and until we meet again, may God hold you in the palm of His hand.

Significance of Family by Robert Childs Jr.

Roberts Jr. is Sandra's oldest brother by her father, Robert, and mother, Annie Bell Childs. I have known Robert Jr. since he was a child and have watched him grow into a fine man with two adult sons. His wife, JoAnn, transition earlier this year. He spoke of the significance of family and the compassion and benevolence of Annie Bell. This same love for family was in Sandra.

Every Easter and Christmas was a time for the gathering of all our families at her home. This happened because of Sandra. Robert Jr. expressed his sincere love for Sandra.

He also gave thanks to me for being a good husband and a friend to his sister. His words were so gracious.

Dignity of Women by Apostle Bam Crawford

Dr. Crawford spoke of the strength of Sandra as a pioneer for justice and dignity of women.

Sandra was a repairer of the breach and was called to raise up many generations of women.

Dr. Crawford spoke of the influence of Sandra in her own life. The teachings on co-equality provoked Dr. Crawford to change her perspective and to even write a book on the topics. She mentioned Sandra as a mentor and as a significant person in the formation of that book and ministry.

Power of the Spirit by Bishop Bill Hamon

Bishop Hamon cited Sandra as a strong prophet who was a keen discerner of gifts, callings and character.

Sandra did not prophesy long prophecies like many of the prophets, for her words were so precious and direct. Sandra was faithful to the Lord, the call and the children.

Bishop Hamon said it is not how long you live but how long you are faithful. He recognized Sandra as a voice for the equality of women and he declared Sandra and Kirby as his friends and member of the leadership of his own ministry.

Significance of Friendship by Dr. Carolyn Driver

Dr. Driver expressed the wonderful friendship she and Sandra experienced. It was one of honesty and purity, and there was never any contention. Sandra was an authentic friend. She spoke of the early days at our home at 3282 Anne Lane Drive when she and Sandra would gather around our dining room table and discuss the gender equality issue.

Sandra was a challenging voice and often would ask why the gender equality issue affected and stirred up so many people. Sandra was a source of mental stimulation in every area of life.

Dr. Driver spoke of the significance of Sandra in her receiving the Baptism in the Holy Spirit. She and Sandra would speak often, and they would even communicate via text messages. She spoke of her last text messages with Sandra, which revealed Sandra's prayer for our family. Sandra texted her and spoke of her health challenges and how God and Kirby kept her alive. Dr. Driver expressed her tremendous loss of her friend and that she was saving those text messages between her and Sandra.

Bishop Kirby Clements Sr. at Sandra's celebration of life, June 2015

How Are You Doing?

Our family has never experienced such a crisis as this. We cannot describe our feelings and the emotions that seem to engulf us at times without notice. Our souls continue to express the consequences of this experience through our tears and unexpected moments of sadness and loneliness. Kirby Jr. and Gina would no longer receive a call or a text message from their mother. They could no longer hear her words of encouragement and wisdom. Sue and Sandra would no longer discuss some of the wonderful ideas and concepts about life. I could no longer hold her or have long conversations with her as we travelled or sat in our home. Our grandchildren would no longer feel her embrace or hear the sound of her voice as she called their names in a particular "grandmotherly fashion." Little Jeffrey at age 4 would not hear grandmother's blessings every morning as she pronounced, "No accidents and no incidents in Jesus name." He is trying to understand why grandmother is not here to hold him and talk with him. Our world has drastically been altered, and there is a part of our lives that is obviously missing.

We receive calls, cards, and text messages with a consistent question: How are you doing? It is a logical question and express-es the concern of so many. We are progressing. We substitute sad thoughts with happy thoughts. Memories are selected based upon their contribution to our emotional and spiritual health. Sandra was vibrant and joyful, and her presence brought life. We thor-oughly gleaned and enjoyed every year of her involvement in our lives. None of us has any regrets, for we have openly talked among ourselves about this. There are no words we wish we had said or wish we had not said. We all feel that the Lord orchestrated a moment in our lives that we could not have done for ourselves. In the presence of our pain, sadness, and loneliness, there remains the emotional partners of love, peace, and confidence. We are pro-gressing because Sandra did not experience pain or distress, and above all, we are progressing because we are assured that this was her time.

Time Is a Healer, Revealer and Concealer

Time is the atmosphere in which we live. As the days, weeks and months progressed, the children and I became more aware of the diminishing of our pain, loss, and loneliness. Kirby Jr., Gina, and Suzette have been a tremendous source of counsel, wisdom, and comfort. During a moment of reflection, Kirby Jr. came into the room and began to talk with me. He reminded me how viewing the videos of Sandra were good memory banks. Even the flowers that we kept from the celebration service were also beautiful memories, but he warned me to be aware that all of these must be held in moderation for they can hinder progress. We will not forget Sandra. How can I forget my love, friend, confident, and companion of over 54 years of life? Nevertheless, I decided to give the ever green flowers to some of our closest friends. This was a moment of healing for me. They could have become a monument and that would not have been good. The time that I decided to give them away was a moment of healing, and it revealed that we were indeed progressing.

Prayer Is for the Living

I generally arise at about 3 in the morning each day in order to pray, study, and write. This has been my pattern for years. Most of the books that Sandra and I wrote were conceived during those early morning hours of meditation. I miss those moments of time with her. We would talk of the things of the Lord and about plans for future ministry. We would pray. My custom has been to give thanks to the Lord for all that He has said and done over these many years. I will not forget the goodness of the Lord and how He providentially directed and guided Sandra and me over the years.

I give thanks to the Lord for Sandra for He gave her a diligent and prevailing spirit. This was so evident through the many years of health and medical challenges and the way Sandra managed the home, dental office, and even the church. Her persistence and willingness to equip other people to be more productive citizens in the Kingdom was most commendable.

One morning during a time of prayer, I was impressed that prayer is for the living. There is no need to make intercession for those who have gone on to glory. We can remember them and give thanks for their lives and contributions. This helped me tremendously. I will give thanks to the Lord for Sandra and the privileges given to both of us. I will give thanks for the many times His providential hand was so obvious in our lives.

During times of prayer in the morning, I would give thanks that the Lord contradicted negative prognoses and even negated the negative side effects of the many medicines that Sandra took daily. Many of them had negative side effects when taken over long periods of time, namely the prednisone, mestinon and others, but the grace of the Lord was so evident. I no longer need to ask for Divine guidance and care for Sandra. I now give thanks and remember the great things the Lord has done. I will give thanks to the Lord, even in this.

Enlarge the Borders of Our Tents

During a time alone in prayer, I was impressed with the passage of Isaiah 54:2:

> *"Enlarge the place of thy tent and let them stretch forth the curtains of thine habitation; spare not, lengthen thy cords, and strengthen thy stakes."*

Borders are physical, psychological, and spiritual. They are beliefs, past experiences, and even people. Age can be a border if you believe that it restricts you and demands your retirement from career activities. Dependency upon a person can be a border since you may have limited yourself because someone else had performed duties that you do not have to do. Sandra was my right hand in every aspect of life.

Early one morning during prayer, I was impressed to enlarge the borders of my life. I was impressed with the idea that you can do a lot of things when you cease to say what you cannot do. As I wrote down my impressions that morning, the following thoughts were so meaningful to me:

*I must speak, but I can choose my words.

*I must listen and hear, but I can choose to believe.

*I must think, but I can choose my thoughts.

*Happiness and sadness are choices.

*Peace is where you put your mind.

These impressions filled my mind and I began to refashion

my attitude and behavior patterns. What Sandra and I had done in our life together, I would now have to do. I realize I must now increase my sensitivity to administrative duties. The borders of my life would increase because now I had to believe that I can do all things. The Spirit of the Lord and the Scriptures would help me. Sandra was gone, and she would not be replaced. As a result, the dimensions of my life would enlarge as I assumed responsibilities that Sandra had performed. The Lord was setting before me greater duties, and they required that I reform my attitude, thoughts, and behavior. I continue to believe that His will never take me and the children where His grace will not keep us.

What If...

Would I desire Sandra back with us again? If so, then I would have to experience the death process again. The children and I are confident that the will of the Lord has been done. Sandra lived her life to the fullest. Nothing restricted her, not even her medical conditions. She never complained of any health issues. She was a life-giver, and everywhere we went, that life energy and purpose were always so obvious in her.

The death certificate said the cause of death was cancer of the lungs, but she was never in pain. The doctors had been unable to detect the problem despite all the tests and medical evaluation. They consistently said that we did nothing wrong. The doctors said the most significant factor was radiation that Sandra received almost forty years ago, from a tumor in her thymus gland.

Our imagination is a powerful tool of creativity. With our imagination, we can change our world and even ourselves. What if the technology in the 1970s was comparable, and the doctors knew what they know today? What if they had only given Sandra the radiation that was necessary? What if, we could change history, then Sandra would be with us today. As these thoughts ran through my mind, I began to imagine so many possibilities. But I knew that regardless of my imagination and any change in history, the will of the Lord would not be changed. The Lord kept us alive all of these years. He had contradicted all the negative prognosis of the doctors and even negated the side effects of the many medicine Sandra had taken for years. The Lord gave us words of hope and life in 1981 that clearly declared that the Lord had the last word in every situation. Sandra and I would often pray together and give thanks to the Lord because He remembered the word upon which He caused us to hope (Psalm 119:49). This was our confidence in the Lord that what He promised we knew He was able to deliver.

With my mind, I know I must think, but I can choose my thoughts. The temptation to imagine what could have been was before me many times. But I find peace in knowing that despite every diagnosis and treatment, that the Lord kept Sandra and sustained her. The children and I do not allow our minds to be tormented with the suggestions of any medical mistakes. We embrace the truth that this was the time and the grace of the Lord was so evident among us. In fact, Kirby Jr. had a dream after the funeral in which his mother appeared and held his hand and confirmed that this was her time and that nothing had been done wrong. The dream was so powerful that when Kirby Jr. had awakened, he felt as if he was still holding Sandra's hand. Our daughter, Gina, had similar impressions of her mother.

CHAPTER 8

A Voice Still Heard and a Presence Still Felt

Sandra was a dedicated student of the Scriptures. Her library was quite extensive and filled with both historic and contemporary books and writings on the issue of creation order. Sandra, in fact, initiated our book titled *And He Gave Them.* She would often share with me topics of research and study regarding the equality of women. I encouraged her to speak often to our local church about her studies. Her teachings opened up treasures of revelation regarding the Kingdom of God and creation order.

The wisdom, knowledge, and counsel of Sandra continues to surface in the testimonies of those who knew her. During an international gathering of leaders from Africa, Asia, Australia, Europe and the United States, several of the speakers expressed their thanksgiving to Sandra for teaching them the principles of creational order and the co-equality of the man and woman in every aspect of life and ministry. Sandra's work on gender was used to support the doctoral work of one our spiritual daughters, Dr. Annyce Stone.

Church leaders, both men and women, cite the teachings and writing of Sandra as a foundation for their government. Parents testify of Sandra's influence in the lives of children during their developmental phases. Her book *Her Name Is Mother* still serves as a tremendous resource to parents who are raising children. Sandra knew the Scriptures revealed examples of women who were business people and who were the head of their household. She taught on the dignity and equality of women from the Scriptures and this amazed many people who consider women to be inferior. A mother and father said when they get in problems with their family they would ask, "what would Pastor Sandra say?" They knew that Sandra was a woman of wisdom and grace. Many would even comment on the Sandra's fashion sense, but they would be quick to say she merged beauty, grace, and wisdom.

Sandra was very industrious. She gained a lot of knowledge and wisdom from her mother, Annie Bell Childs, who was a very effective entrepreneur. Sandra merged beauty and intelligence when she and our daughter, Gina, started their own cosmetic company. The company provided cosmetic products and beauty tips. Sandra and Gina would provide mini beauty seminars at our home, outside venues and even at my dental office. In fact, the seminars at my dental office were so popular and successful that we merged cosmetics and dentistry. Perhaps, we were the pioneers of the early phases of cosmetic and esthetic dentistry that is today so popular.

The Books

The role of women in the church, home and market place was a significant concern for Sandra. Her study of the Scriptures and unlimited resources of reading material was an expression of her dedication to the topic of co-laborship. Because Sandra was known as a pioneer for justice regarding the role of women, people would send her books on creational order. She studied diligently and recorded all of her notes in a large binder. We decided to consolidate her notes and teaching material into a book. I remember the day we were deliberating on the title and immediately the thought came to us. The book was to be titled *And He Gave Them*. After all, in Genesis 1:26, it clearly states that in creation the Lord gave *them* the commission. This book was our inaugural project, and it served as a tremendous source of information, wisdom, and insight. We decided that we should both be the authors. While Sandra wrote on topics such as the Genesis story, headship, covering, submission, and examples of women in both the Old and New Testament, I covered topics such gender, religion, and science. We put together work books that further expanded the information.

Sandra wrote other books that expanded on the role of women in the home. One of the treasure of her writing is recorded in her book entitled, *Her Name Is Mother*. This book offers practical insight, wisdom, and knowledge on the role of women in parenting and the care of themselves. We followed this book with one titled *Spiritual Intelligence,* which provided understanding of difficult Scriptures and words such as head, helpmeet, submission, silence, and authority.

These writings provided the foundation for many opportunities to teach on the topic of gender. Although Sandra was the driving force, our labor together was a tremendous statement since it demonstrated the principle of co-laborship. Sandra's presence in meetings was recognized as a statement of co-laborship. Once in an international conference in England with leaders from Africa, Asia, Europe, South and North America, Australia, and the Caribbean, one of the major speaker openly apologized for the negligence of the conference to include women as speakers. The motivation for his comment was the presence of Sandra in the audience.

Pioneer for Justice and Equality

Sandra was never a conformist, and she had a passion for the justice, dignity and liberty of women. She never accepted the social stereotype of women as inferior citizens. We always had an egalitarian relationship. We both loved and respected one another. There was never a debate over rights and privileges based upon gender. When we came into the church, we faced issue of male headship and female submission. There was strong teaching by the church leadership that men ruled over women. Sandra knew this was a misrepresentation of the character of God. As a result of her position, she studied the Scriptures and numerous books and publications on the subject of gender. She was so diligent in her quest for revelation and knowledge on the topic. She met and was encouraged by Daisy Osborn, world renowned evangelist and wife of T.L. Osborn. Daisy was also a pioneer for the rights of women. As a result of Sandra's diligence, we wrote our book, *And He Gave Them,* which set forth the co-equality of men and women in the church, home and market place. We organized seminars and taught extensively from our book. Church leaders, business people and students would attend the seminars. The years of research, study and prayer produced wonderful results as we dealt with the Scriptures and historic writings. Once after one of our seminars in Australia, the host leader who had invited us, immediately ordained three women to the ministry. And today those three women are some of the most powerful ministers in that organization.

Our seminars were not without challenge. As already mentioned, during one of our meetings in England, there was such a tremendous response from the congregation. The women in the church were not allowed to function as preacher and teacher. But as Sandra taught from the Scriptures and addressed the source of the misconception of female submission and male domination, the wives of the leaders and the congregation were so excited. However, the male-dominated leadership was threatened and requested that we not teach or distribute our book.

During a subsequent ministry trip to England, Sandra spoke on co-equality and gender and it really challenged the status quo of the ministry. Women were not allowed to minister and were not part of the eldership. That morning during our last session, we offered a time of prayer for the people. Many of them flooded the altar area and the men were trying to minister to them. However, there were so many people and the men were attempting to pray long prayers over each one of them. Sandra and I asked the wives of the men and some of the other women to join in the ministry of prayer. They moved among the people with such grace and power and you could see the fruitfulness of their ministry as people were healed. Some of the people shouted with joy over the words of knowledge and wisdom given to them by the women and many were literally slain in the spirit. The men continued to labor while the women were triumphant. They came and the power of God was manifested as people received the Holy Spirit and were healed of infirmities.

Shortly after that ministry session, the elders had a meeting with us and requested us not to teach any more on creational order and to discontinue selling *And He Gave Them*, which was a discourse on role of men and women in the church, market place, and the home. While we obeyed their request, the effect of our ministry had already taken effect. The women desired to know more about our book on gender in Scripture.

During a ministry trip to El Salvador, Sandra and I taught creation order and the Divine job description given to the man and the woman. We proved by Scripture that both the man and woman were made in the image of God and that the woman was not cursed. The response was tremendous. Our teachings challenged the oppression of women and even uncovered the fundamental reason behind adultery among many of the men. During a teaching session, Sandra declared that any man who abuses his wife physically or emotionally is not a Christian. Her teachings struck at the heart of much of the relationship crises in the country. In fact, a prophetic word was given through us that a day would come when a woman would be the chief political officer in that country. Years later, it came to pass.

Sandra never relented when teachings were presented that she deemed contrary to Scripture regarding women. Once during a conference in California, a noted minister openly taught that God imparts revelation first to the man, and then the man imparts it to the woman. Sandra was enraged, and when her time came to minister, she openly declared that anyone who sets forth a principle of male domination and any idea that God speaks to the man first and then to the woman, is teaching a doctrine born out of hell.

Sandra was truly a pioneer for justice.

We visited South Africa again during the apartheid regime. We were invited by the largest Pentecostal organization in the country, and they scheduled us to teach in their churches and their Bible School. Our teaching on the Kingdom of God and creational order was revolutionary. During one of our meetings in the Bible School, two young men entered the meeting. Their presence created quite a bit of unrest among the students. We would later discover that they were members of the African National Congress, a group of South African leaders and people who embraced liberation theology and the use of violence to overthrow the apartheid government. One of them asked if he could make a statement. He addressed the evil of the government and asked if violence was a political and social option. When we spoke of the ethical and moral demands of the Kingdom of God and how the church was supposed to be a standard of righteousness, they were shocked and encouraged. The doctrine of the Pentecostal churches had taught that salvation was soul winning and church planting and going to heaven. No concern was given to cultural transformation. In fact, as Sandra and I taught on the Kingdom of God, the leaders of the church accused us of "politicizing the church." Nevertheless, we persisted.

We were invited to South Africa a second time to speak to the first international gathering of the four factions of the church. For the first time in the history of the organization, the Blacks, Colored,

Indian and Afrikaner groups would meet together. Sandra and I were the first African-Americans ever invited to speak to such a gathering. During our time there, Sandra met with a large gathering of the women of the organization. Her teaching on co-equality generated an overwhelming response from the women. The women wept openly as they realized the truth of the Scriptures. Needless to say, the male leaders were upset. Nevertheless, the grace of the Lord was so mightily upon us that the male leaders, despite their objections, opened more doors for us to speak.

Sandra and I were invited to minister in a Baptist Church in Alabama. We did not know that women had never been allowed in the pulpit of that church. Well, when I was presented to preach that morning, I escorted Sandra to the pulpit to speak before I would preach. Sandra's words were so accurate and addressed critical issues involving the church at that moment. The elders and the congregation were in awe at the preciseness of her words regarding the history of the church and even future decisions and plans. Once we finished ministering and were speaking to the people and elders, we were made aware that this was the first time in the history of the church that a woman had been allowed to stand behind the pulpit or even preach. Yet, Sandra's words were precise and informative that even the elders and congregation began to ask questions about creation order.

Ministry delegation in El Salvador, 2002

Teaching women in Korea, May 2014

Praying over young souls in Korea, May 2014

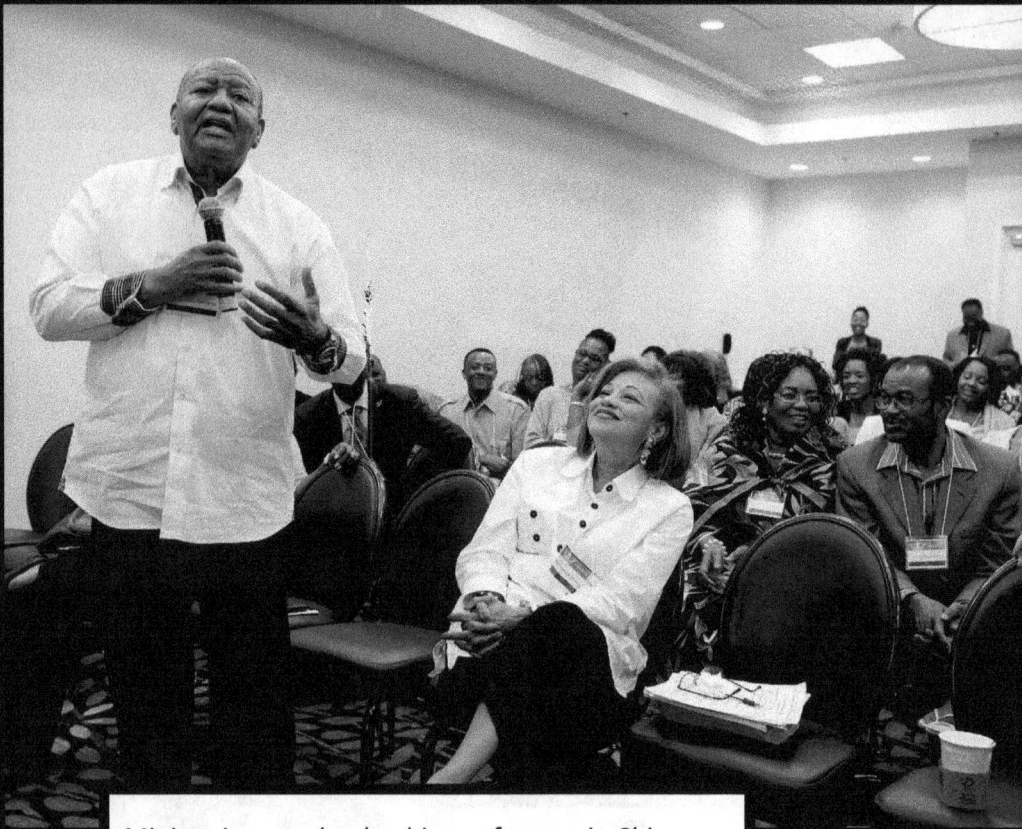
Ministering at a leadership conference in Chicago

California ministry team, July 2013

Ministry conference in England, December 2014

Ministry conference in Brussels, December 2014

Sandra speaking a ministry in California

CHAPTER 9

A New World

Fifteen years ago, I received a book written by Dr. T.L. Osborn, a Pentecostal evangelist who had preached in over 81 nations and to some of the largest crowds ever recorded. T.L. had lost his wife, Daisy, after 52 years of marriage. Daisy and T.L. had been inseparable in life and ministry. Daisy was the organizer and frontrunner in the ministry. She planned crusades and coordinated meetings with leaders and officials. Daisy was a tremendous teacher and held conferences that promoted the dignity and liberty of women.

When Daisy had passed away, T.L. wrote a book titled *Why?: Tragedy, Trauma, Triumph*. The book is a record of his life after the death of his beloved Daisy. When I received the book 15 years ago and became aware of its content, I refused to read it. It possessed too many strong suggestions that I might experience, such a tragedy. But now, on the morning after the transition of my

Sandra, I read the book and wept as I absorbed the grief of T.L. He wrote that the landscape of his life had changed and that he only knew himself in partnership with Daisy. He did not know T.L. Osborn, the widower. His words struck at the core of my heart when he wrote, "We lost our Daisy, but we did not lose ourselves." My children and I have lost a tremendous part of our existence, but we have not lost ourselves.

Nevertheless, we cannot allow our grief, sorrow or pain to cancel our lives. As a family, we have decided we would gather strength from our many memories. Technology is beautiful in this regard. We viewed video recordings of Sandra teaching. She and I labored together, so we had many video recordings of our teaching sessions together. We had taken a family photographs just the year prior to our loss and those pictures had been framed and available to all of us. Sandra is present even though she is absent. I can neither touch her beautiful face nor have our long talks together about things of God and the issues of life, but I have memories! And memories are like currency that purchase hope, peace, and confidence in the future. There were no regrets and no unfinished business. There were no words we wished we had shared with Sandra. There are no historic moments that any of us dread or wish we could change. Our memory banks are filled with wonderful and beautiful treasures of pictures, experiences, and recordings of her. As T.L. decided to continue life and ministry without Daisy, we decided to continue life and ministry without our beloved Sandra. We are called of God, and there is unfinished work to be done.

Even within the confines of our decision, each day passing was a challenge to us. Our emotions of grief, loss, and loneliness would sweep over us like waves of water. At times, it appeared that we were powerless to resist the sadness and sense of loss. We knew this was a part of the grief process, and we were not trying to resist. Sandra was part of my life for 54 years. Our children, Kirby Jr. and Gina, love their mother dearly and rarely missed a day talking with her. Our lives had been altered, and we had no memories of such an experience. The beauty of the crisis was that my children, and I shared it together. Each of us could understand the pain and distress of one another. We would huddle together and sometimes weep and console each other.

Alone but Continuing

As I walk through our home, I see Sandra's influence and her creativity in the furniture, pictures, and the walls that are draped with beautiful blue plates. Sandra loved blue, and our walls are filled with these beautiful ceramic plates that we collected during our many national and international travels. The shelves on the walls are filled with beautiful artifacts and collections of art that Sandra collected over nearly 50 years. I cannot enter our bedroom without sensing her presence. I have allowed all things to remain as they were since the morning we left for her medical treatment. Her clothes are still arranged in the closet as only Sandra could have arranged them. I know the time will come when I will make all the changes necessary. But this is a personal journey and the comfort of the Scriptures, beautiful memories, and the arrangement of our home are a comfort.

The children and I often talk about her and the many experiences. As times passes, we discover and express the many conversations we had with Sandra. These are wonderful moments even though they are sprinkled with pain and loss. But there is no regret or feelings of anything that should have been said or done. We only miss her so much. Sandra is present even when she is absent. She is a part of our transcendent team with one member being in heaven and one on earth. We experience her influence in our lives every moment. When I walk through the rooms of our home, I see Sandra with her grace and knowledge of beauty, order, and design. Her wisdom and discernment is often expressed in the decisions and choices that we make in every aspect of our lives. Like all pioneers and prophets, Sandra's words and influence are still among us. We truly thank the Lord for these wonderful memories.

Being alone, this is a totally new experience for me. I am a widower. Although our grown children with their families are a part of our household, I am alone. My pain, grief, and loneliness paralyzes me at times. I know with the passing of time that these emotions will not be as powerful. But each day I choose my thoughts and memories. I continue with our work in ministry and dentistry. Sandra was a most significant part of all of this. We made decisions together about every aspect of life and now she is not here. She was my life, light, joy, excitement, counselor, friend, and intimate mate for more than 50 years. I had never been without her except for a few days or a week when I travelled to another country where she could not go because of the heat. The hot weather would always make her weak, so we decided we would not endanger her health. When I was away, I would call her several times during the day. Our faith was in God, and this was wisdom.

Now when I arrive home, there is no Sandra. Loneliness is like an oppression. I constantly draw upon my memory bank. I did not allow her departure to stop me, though. Family and friends alike told me to take time off from work, but that was not the impression in my heart. While my grief, pain, and loneliness are companions, they must be with me as I continue in the work the Lord gave us – and now me – to do.

My children and I spend a lot of time talking about Sandra. We are not in any denial, for we know our pain is real. It cannot go away quickly, and there is neither a place to go to avoid it nor a substitute to be found in anything. Thus, we talk and we cry, and at times, we laugh. We know that each succeeding day will be different. When the days turn into weeks, months and years, there will be our memories without the same dimension of pain and loneliness. Each day, I see and experience her influence in our home with all of its beautiful decorations and pictures. I am currently revising some of our books to ensure that the material on the Kingdom of God and creational order is preserved and available more readily.

Every morning, I awake and give thanks to the Lord for His grace, mercy and favor. I read and listen to the Scriptures and pray in my language and in tongues. I remind myself of His promises and give thanks on what He has done for all creation and for us.

His Promises

He promised to give us *beauty for ashes*, the *oil of joy* for mourning and *garment of praise* for the spirit of heaviness (Isaiah 61:3). For sadness and sorrow, He will give joy and peace. By His grace, we will complete our course and fulfill His mandate. Sandra and I are a transcendent team with one in heaven and the other on earth. Precious memories, pictures, videos and books testify to over a half century of life together. I listen and watch videos of our ministry together. Some of them are recorded on YouTube. In my mind and heart, she remains an ambassador for justice. The Lord's promise kept us these many years, and His word now sustains us. We will be fine.

I have choices. I could choose to allow grief to overwhelm me and even quit on life and ministry. I could become a recluse and close off all our friends and even family. But I discovered that life is a choice. I am discovering Kirby without Sandra. I am still needed in the Kingdom of God. The wisdom and knowledge that is given to me is still needed. There are more books to be written, and there are countries and nations for me to visit that I have never visited before. And beside all of this, my children and grandchildren need me. I must continue to be dad and grandad to them all.

After Sandra's transition, the pain and loneliness have been overwhelming. Bishop Bill Hamon spoke openly to me while he was ministering in a local church one day. He said the Lord has given me the Spirit of wisdom and revelation, strength, and a special measure of grace for this next phase of life and ministry. We are to war a good warfare according to the prophecies that we receive. This word and the many impressions and promises that I have received from the Lord are the source of my confidence and joy.

Choosing to Live

Life and death are common experiences shared by all. There have been many who have shared my experience of loss and loneliness. I am surrounded by a great cloud of witnesses who have withstood every challenge of life to fulfill their ministry. My life belongs to the Lord. The ministry that Sandra and I shared together for all these years is larger than my personal life. Would I want Sandra back again? Then I would have to experience the pain of separation again. Sandra was my love, companion, and the joy of my life. There is no need for another companion. At 74 years of age, all of my needs for life and companionship were fulfilled with my Sandra. I now choose to live and fulfill my ministry with joy.

The words of Paul are an encouragement to me (Acts 20:24). I am writing this work, for it will be a source of hope, inspiration, and courage to those who read it. It is a God story. His will never takes you where His grace will not keep you. The finish line is a long way away for me. Sandra finished her course. Her legacy is beautiful. She was joy, hope, confidence, encouragement, counsel, and strength for many. She was the love of my life. Whenever and wherever I travel, I will preach some for Sandra. I teach about the Kingdom of God and creational order. His grace is always sufficient. And we have no controversy. But above all, God has no controversy with us.

Lounging at home on the porch

Worshipping at their home church, The Community of the Holy Spirit

Hosting ministry partners from Africa at home

Sandra and Kirby Sr., together teaching in their ministry

Sandra enjoying a moment during a ministry trip to Korea in 2014

The Books

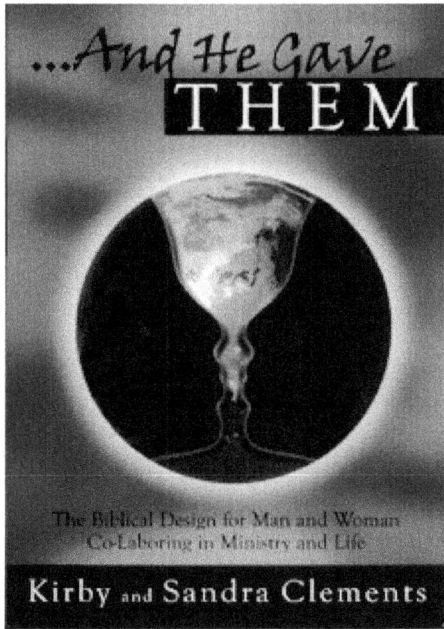

...And He Gave THEM

The Biblical Design for Man and Woman
Co-Laboring in Ministry and Life

Kirby and Sandra Clements

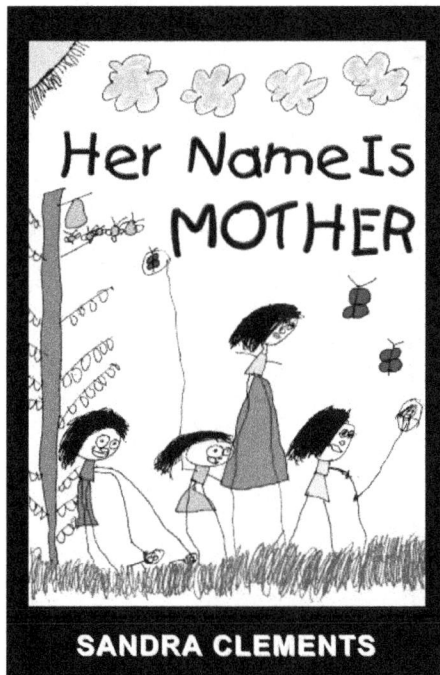

Her Name Is MOTHER

SANDRA CLEMENTS

SPIRITUAL INTELLIGENCE
Knowing God and Making Him Known

Kirby and Sandra Clements

Prevailing Spirit
A Journal of Survival

SANDRA
CLEMENTS

www.ingramcontent.com/pod-product-compliance
Lightning Source LLC
Chambersburg PA
CBHW062010040426
42447CB00010B/1994